LATINO LIFE

SPEAKING TWO LANGUAGES

SPEAKING TWO LANGUAGES

by Bethanie L. Boswell

Rourke Publications, Inc.

The following sources are acknowledged and thanked for the use of their photographs in this work: Jim Whitmer pp. 2, 26, 45; Richard B. Levine p. 8; Bob Daemmrich pp. 10, 11; Gail Denham p. 17; Claire Rydell p. 19; Frances M. Roberts pp. 20, 37, 38; Envision/ MacDonald Photography p. 22; Cindy Reiman/Impact Visuals p. 28; PmPorter/Don Franklin p. 31; Hazel Hankin p. 33; AP/Wide World Photos p. 41. Maps on pp. 7, 14, and 23 by Moritz Design.

Produced by Salem Press, Inc.

Copyright © 1995, by Rourke Publications, Inc.

Library of Congress Cataloging-in-Publication Data
Boswell, Bethanie L., 1972-
    Speaking two languages / by Bethanie L. Boswell.
        p.   cm. — (Latino life)
    ISBN 0-86625-543-5
    1. Hispanic Americans—Juvenile literature. 2. Education, Bilingual—United States—Juvenile literature. 3. Bilingualism— United States—Juvenile literature. [1. Hispanic Americans. 2. Bilingualism.] I. Title. II. Series.
E184.S75B68   1995
973'.0468—dc20   95-2016
                                       CIP
                                        AC

1/97

First Printing

PRINTED IN THE UNITED STATES OF AMERICA

CONTENTS

Chapter 1

SPANISH COMES TO AMERICA

Spanish-speaking people have been very important in the *culture* of the United States. Before the United States was a country, Spanish settlers built small towns in southern California, Arizona, New Mexico, Texas, and northern Mexico. This part of North America is known as the *Southwest*. The Spanish language became the most important language in the Southwest. Later, new settlers came to the Southwest, and they spoke English. English became important, too, but Spanish stayed the *first language*, or *primary language*, for many people in the Southwest. Today it is still very important.

People who speak Spanish have also come to the United States from other countries, like Mexico, Puerto Rico, and Cuba. Sometimes they come to find better jobs and make more money. Sometimes they come from countries where wars are happening. Whatever reasons they have for coming to the United States, Spanish speakers improve our country and make it stronger.

THE SPANISH COME TO THE NEW WORLD

In 1492, Christopher Columbus, an Italian sailor, led several boats of men from Spain to the North American continent. He was looking for China. Instead, he had reached the New World. He claimed its land for Spain. His trips started Europe's exploration of the New World.

Spanish Exploration in the New World

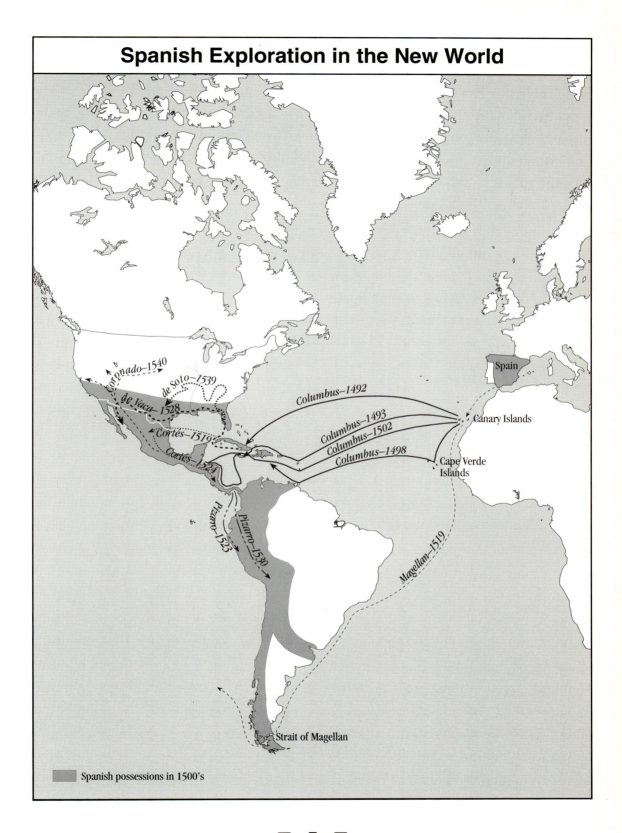

Spain

Canary Islands

Cape Verde Islands

Columbus–1492

Columbus–1493

Columbus–1502

Columbus–1498

Magellan–1519

Coronado–1540

de Soto–1539

de Vaca–1528

Cortés–1519

Cortés–1521

Pizarro–1523

Pizarro–1530

Strait of Magellan

Spanish possessions in 1500's

Spain was the first country to send men on horses to North America to explore the newly discovered land. Another Spanish explorer, Hernando de Soto, looked for gold. From 1539 to 1541, he explored the land from Florida west to the Mississippi River. From 1540 to 1542, the explorer Francisco Vásquez de Coronado explored territory in Texas, Kansas, New Mexico, and Arizona.

SPAIN IN THE SOUTHWEST

In the Southwest, the first settlers from Europe were also from Spain. Juan de Oñate led one group of these settlers. They built small towns in the Southwest in the early 1600's. Another group of Spanish settlers was living in Mexico. It was difficult to get to California from the towns in Mexico. Spanish settlers did not live in California until the 1700's.

In the 1700's, a priest named Father Junípero Serra and an expedition leader named Don Gaspar de Portolá started a

Early Spanish settlers built churches and missions throughout the Southwestern United States.

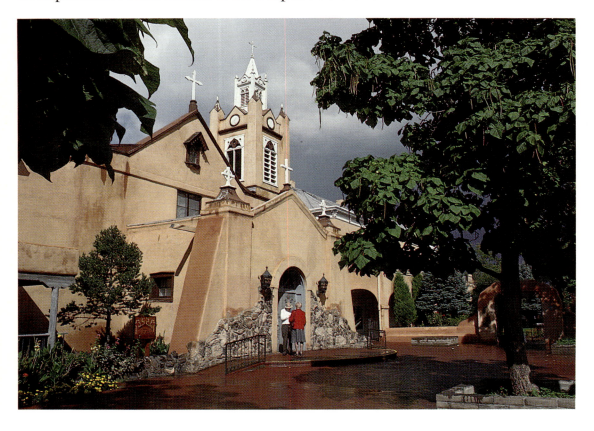

big project. With the help of the Indians who lived in California, they built missions all along the California coast. Each mission was like a small town with a Catholic church. The missions began at San Diego and ended at San Francisco. You can still visit them today.

The road between the missions has a Spanish name, El Camino Real. It means The Royal Highway. A car trip from one end to the other end takes about ten hours. Imagine how long it took in a wagon pulled by animals!

THE UNITED STATES GROWS UP—AND OUT

In 1783, the American colonists won the War for Independence against the British, and the United States was born. It took a long time for the new country to set up a government. It took even longer to settle the rest of the country. When the Founding Fathers wrote the Constitution in 1787, the country reached only to the Mississippi River. That is less than one-third the size of the country today. California, Arizona, New Mexico, Texas, and parts of other states belonged to the Spanish.

OTHER SPANISH SPEAKERS IN THE UNITED STATES

The Spanish settled most of Central and South America, spreading their language as they went. Today, most of the people in Central and South America speak Spanish as their primary language. There are quite a few countries where Spanish is the primary language. The United States and these countries are close neighbors. It is no wonder that, in the United States, Spanish is spoken more than any other language except English.

Spanish-speaking people in the United States mainly come from three countries: Mexico, Puerto Rico, and Cuba. These countries are closer to the United States than most of the other Spanish-speaking countries. In fact, being close to the United States is an important reason people come here.

This sign, in English and Spanish, marks the U.S.-Mexican border. The populations of Mexico, Cuba, and Puerto Rico speak Spanish, and many people come to the United States from these locations.

MEXICAN IMMIGRATION

Most Spanish speakers in the United States are Mexican Americans. They make up more than half of all Spanish speakers in the country. So many Mexicans come to America because Mexico is very close to the United States. The two countries share a long border that runs between Mexico and the U.S. states of California, Arizona, New Mexico, and Texas. It is not a very long trip from Mexico to the United States.

PUERTO RICANS ON THE MAINLAND

Puerto Ricans have come to America from Puerto Rico. Puerto Rico is an island in the Caribbean Sea. Puerto Rico is not a separate country. It is part of the United States. It is easier for Puerto Ricans to come into the United States than it is for other Spanish speakers, because Puerto Ricans are already U.S. *citizens*. Puerto Ricans can come into the United States and return to Puerto Rico as often as they like. Many Puerto Ricans come to the United States to make a better living. There are more jobs for Puerto Ricans in the United States, and they can earn more money.

CUBAN IMMIGRATION

Cubans come to the United States from the country of Cuba. Like Puerto Rico, Cuba is an island in the Caribbean Sea. Unlike Puerto Rico, Cuba is not part of the United States. It is another country. Today, people are not allowed to travel back and forth between the United States and Cuba because of disagreements between our governments. Cuban people still try to get to America, though. Often they come in boats. They can do this because Cuba is very close to the coast of Florida. It is only ninety miles away.

Most people have come to the United States from Cuba in the last thirty-five years. In 1959, a man named Fidel Castro took over the Cuban government. In the early years, Castro did some good things for the Cuban people, but he eventually took away many of their rights. Many Cubans left the island to get to the United States.

Before 1991, Cuba sold crops to the Soviet Union. The Soviet Union was a very big country that contained Russia and part of Asia. The Soviet Union would buy Cuba's crops, and Cubans would get the money. The Cuban government used the money to build schools and hospitals for the people.

In 1991, the Soviet Union fell apart. It became a group of smaller countries, including Russia. Russia and the other small countries did not have extra money to buy Cuba's crops. Cuba became poorer and poorer. It became harder for Cubans to find jobs and earn enough money to live. Even more Cubans tried to enter the United States.

OTHER SPANISH SPEAKERS

Most Spanish speakers in the United States come from Mexico, Puerto Rico, and Cuba, but they come from many other countries, too. They also come from Central American countries like Guatemala, Honduras, and Nicaragua. When there are wars in other countries, many people in those countries try to leave and go somewhere else until the war is over. These people are called *refugees*.

Some of the people who come from Central America are refugees trying to save their lives. Others are trying to find better jobs to earn more money for their families.

El Paso, Texas, is one of many U.S. border towns with a large Spanish-speaking population.

Whatever their reasons for coming to America, all these Spanish-speaking people have made American culture better. The United States was built on new ideas brought from other countries. *Immigrants*—people who come from other countries to live in America—bring new ideas and new traditions. They make American life more interesting. As long as new people bring these new ideas to America, the country will keeping getting stronger.

Chapter 2

SPANISH AND ENGLISH

Spanish and English may seem like very different languages, but in some ways they are a lot alike. Spanish and English both belong to what is called the *Indo-European family of languages.*

WE ARE FAMILY: THE INDO-EUROPEAN LANGUAGES

More people speak languages from the Indo-European family than any other family of languages. About half of the world's people speak an Indo-European language. People who live in Russia, the United States, and almost all of Europe and South America speak Indo-European languages.

All of the Indo-European languages have things in common. They have different words for the same things, but sometimes these words sound alike. For instance, the English word for "mother" in Russian is *mat* (sounds like *maht*). In Spanish, "mother" is *madre* (sounds like *MAHdray*). *Moth*er and *mat* and *ma*dre sound alike. Say them aloud and you'll see.

These "sound-alike" words are called *cognates.* Even though English is closer to German and Spanish is closer to languages like French and Italian, they both are close to a language called *Latin.* English has many words that come from Latin. Spanish gets most of its words from Latin. When there is a word in one language that is very close to

Spanish-Speaking Countries

United States

Mexico

Cuba

Haiti

Dominican Republic

Belize

Guatemala

Honduras

El Salvador

Nicaragua

Costa Rica

Panama

Colombia

Venezuela

Guyana

Suriname

French Guiana

Ecuador

Peru

Brazil

Bolivia

Chile

Paraguay

Uruguay

Argentina

Spain

that word in another language, the words usually sound alike. Spanish and English share many cognates.

IMPORTANT DIFFERENCES BETWEEN THE LANGUAGES

Spanish and English are also different. One of the biggest differences between Spanish and English is *gender*. In Spanish, words for things are either male or female, like *el libro* or *la casa*. *El* is the male form of "the." *La* is the female form of "the." English uses words like *the book* and *the house*. The word "the" remains the same; it has no gender.

Another difference between Spanish and English is word order. In English, the adjective (the descriptive word) is usually put *in front of* the noun (the thing that it is describing): the *tall* boy, the *red* ball. In Spanish, the adjective is usually placed *after* the noun: el muchacho *alto*, la pelota *roja*.

Words and letters are also pronounced differently in Spanish. In English, the letter *e* can be pronounced *ee* as in *tree*, or *eh* as in *pet*. In English, if you put *e* together with an *a* or an *i*, you get completely different sounds. In Spanish, if you have an *e*, you will always say it with an *ay* sound, as in *day*. An *a* always sounds like the *ah* in *mama*, and *i* always sounds like the *ee* in *tree*.

Also, Spanish words sometimes use accent marks to help people read the words aloud: *corazón* (heart), *Martínez* (a name), *árbol* (tree). When people see this accent mark, they speak that part of the word a little harder and louder.

BREAKING THROUGH THE LANGUAGE WALL

Even if two people do not speak the same language, they can *communicate*. Talking is one important way of communicating. There are also other ways. Using hand signals or body language—like waving, shrugging your shoulders, smiling, or rolling your eyes toward the ceiling— are other ways to "talk" to another person. You could also draw pictures to show what you mean.

Think about how a traffic light communicates to people. It never says a word, but when there is a red light, all the cars stop. When the light turns green, the cars go again. Sometimes people can communicate the same way. No matter what language you speak, a smile always says something nice to other people.

IT'S A SMALL WORLD AFTER ALL

Most of the languages in the world are from the Indo-European family. Among those languages there are many differences, but there are also many similarities. Spanish and English share many cognates. If you learn some of these sound-alike words, you can start to become *bilingual*. *Bi* means "two," and *lingual* means "language."

Cognates in English and Spanish	
English	**Spanish**
baseball	béisbol
cafeteria	cafetería
excellent	excelente
football	fútbol
grand, large, big	grande
liberty	libertad
mathematics	matemáticas
office	oficina
simply	simplemente
student	estudiante
stupendous	estupendo
terrible	terrible
to comprehend	comprender
to castigate, to punish	castigar
vacation	vacaciones

*When you
can speak both
Spanish and
English, you
can communicate
with many more
people.*

"Bilingual" means that you can speak two languages. When you can speak both English and Spanish, you can learn to communicate with many, many people. When you are bilingual, it really is a small world after all.

Chapter 3

WHO SPEAKS SPANISH?

We have talked about some different places where people speak Spanish before coming to the United States: Mexico, Puerto Rico, and Cuba, for example. Now we are going to see where these Spanish speakers live after they move to the United States.

SPANISH SPEAKERS IN THE SOUTHWEST

Mexican Americans are the largest group of Spanish speakers in the United States. Mexico is just south of the United States, and the two countries share a border that is roughly 1,500 miles long. As you might guess, Mexican Americans live mostly in the American Southwest: California, Arizona, New Mexico, and Texas.

Spanish settlers from the south were the first people to settle the Southwest. Spanish speakers settled the Southwest long before the United States was a country. There were many Spanish-speaking ranchers. They named many of the cities and streets in the Southwest. That is why many places in California, Texas, Arizona, New Mexico, and other states have Spanish names: San Francisco, San Antonio, La Jolla, El Camino Real, El Paso, Santa Fe. This list goes on and on.

The Spanish settlers who lived in the Southwest sometimes married the Indians. Their children stayed in the Southwest. In the 1840's and 1850's, European Americans came from the East to settle in the West. By then, the

Spanish speakers in the Southwest come mainly from Mexico or have ancestors who were Mexican.

Spanish-speaking settlers had lived in the Southwest for many generations. The United States took the land away from Spain and Mexico, but some of the Spanish speakers stayed in their homeland. Now they were living in the United States, but they still spoke Spanish.

Today, the long border between Mexico and the United States makes it easy to enter the United States. People come to the United States from Mexico to get jobs. Farms in California and Texas need people to work in the fields and harvest the crops. Immigrants can find jobs that pay better than the ones they had in Mexico. They hope to enroll their children in the public schools. Earning more money and giving their children an education helps immigrants to build a better life in the United States.

SPANISH SPEAKERS IN NEW YORK

Many Puerto Ricans who come to the United States settle in New York City and areas nearby. In fact, more Puerto Ricans live in New York than live in San Juan, the capital city of Puerto Rico!

Puerto Ricans live in New York for two reasons. First, it is easy to get to New York by flying in an airplane. During World War II (1941-1945), airplanes were built for war. After the war, the airplanes were not being used. The airplane companies decided to use the airplanes to move people instead of guns, tanks, and troops. Before the war ended, it was rare to travel by plane. People had to travel by train or by ship. That could be very expensive and very tiring. Traveling by plane took less time. After the war, Puerto Ricans came to New York in airplanes, and many Puerto Ricans made New York their home.

Puerto Ricans had another reason to move to New York. In New York City, they could find jobs. The jobs that they found in the city paid better money than jobs they had in Puerto Rico. Even when Puerto Ricans could not find good jobs, the jobs they did get were better than the jobs they could find in Puerto Rico.

In the Northeast, especially in New York City, Spanish speakers are often from Puerto Rico.

SPANISH SPEAKERS IN FLORIDA

Most Cuban Americans live in southern Florida. Like the Puerto Ricans who moved to New York City, Cubans moved to a big city. Cubans moved to Miami, a large city in Florida. Miami is the closest big city to the country of Cuba.

Cubans moved to the United States for several reasons. Sometimes, they disagreed with the Cuban government. If they spoke too much about these feelings, they might be put in jail. These people had to escape just because of their beliefs. (The first European settlers in America, the Pilgrims, left Europe for the same reason.)

Spanish speakers also come from Cuba to escape poverty. Cuba has become a very poor country in the last few years. It is hard for people to find jobs that pay enough money to buy food. Even when people have enough money to buy food, the stores may have no food to sell to them.

These Cuban American businessmen sell shoes in Miami's "Little Havana," which is heavily populated with Cubans and Cuban Americans.

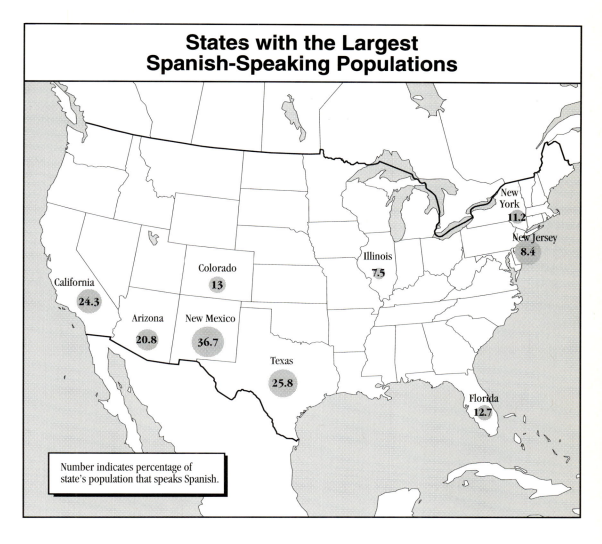

States with the Largest Spanish-Speaking Populations

New York 11.2

New Jersey 8.4

Illinois 7.5

Colorado 13

California 24.3

Arizona 20.8

New Mexico 36.7

Texas 25.8

Florida 12.7

Number indicates percentage of state's population that speaks Spanish.

BUILDING COMMUNITIES

Spanish speakers often settle in places where other Spanish speakers live. Often, they choose to live with other people from their country. Mexican immigrants might live in the same neighborhood as other Mexicans. Cubans might decide to live in a neighborhood where other Cubans live. They form a *community*. A community is a group of people with the same background who live together in a neighborhood.

Communities grow slowly, over a long period of time. Some of the first Puerto Ricans to come to America went to New York because they could get jobs there. After those first Puerto Ricans moved into New York, they found places to live. Now it was easier for more people from Puerto Rico to move to New York. They could stay with their friends and relatives who had already found homes and jobs there.

People become part of a community because they share the same language and culture. People who live in a community together often help each other find jobs. They can tell new neighbors where there are good stores for shopping. If the stores do not sell their special foods or clothes, they can start their own stores. Soon new businesses grow. New restaurants appear. More friends and neighbors from the old country move to the new country. The new community has become a friendly and familiar place.

We all live in one sort of community or another. We all help the people with whom we share our neighborhoods.

Chapter 4

The Bilingual Education Act of 1968

Today, children in the United States come from many different places. Because children come from different places and speak different languages, the Bilingual Education Act was passed in 1968. This law says that *non-English-speaking* and *limited-English-speaking* children in the United States have certain rights. Children who do not speak English have the right to be taught in the language they know best. They also have the right to be helped to learn English.

Bilingual Education before World War I

Before World War I (1914-1918), children in the United States were often taught in their own languages. For example, German immigrants taught their children in schools where German was spoken. Where Chinese people lived, children learned in Chinese. When World War I started, speaking, teaching, and learning only English became an important way of showing *patriotism*. Patriotism is love for the country in which you live. Many people thought that all U.S. citizens should show their patriotism by speaking English only, because English is the language that most U.S. citizens speak.

This idea that only English should be used in schools was popular among schools until the 1960's. In the 1960's, many Spanish-speaking immigrants began moving into Florida. They sent their children to American schools. Suddenly there were many people who did not speak English. The schools in Florida decided to teach the children in their own language, Spanish. Teaching children in Spanish also became popular in New Mexico and Texas. New Mexico and Texas had large Spanish-speaking populations.

This way of teaching was called "bilingual education." At the end of Chapter 2, we learned that *bilingual* means "two languages." *Bilingual education* means "learning in two languages." It also means that some classrooms may have children who speak only English and other children who speak only Spanish. The teachers help the Spanish-speaking children learn their lessons in Spanish, but the children learn English, too.

WHY THE LAW WAS PASSED

Many teachers and parents liked this way of teaching in two languages. The children were able to learn English, the main language of their new country. At the same time, they could learn their regular lessons—arithmetic, reading, and writing—in their primary language, Spanish. That way, they did not get behind while they were learning the new language.

More people began to like bilingual education, so in 1968 Congress passed the Bilingual Education Act. The law gave schools money to start bilingual programs. The law helped all children who could not speak English. It helped the children by teaching them in their first language, the language they know best.

BILINGUAL EDUCATION HELPS

To understand how helpful bilingual education is, try to imagine how difficult it would be to learn if your teacher tried to teach you in a language that you did not know. It

The Bilingual Education Act says that children who do not speak English well have a right to be helped to learn it.

would be hard to understand what the words meant. Trying to learn something new, like adding or subtracting, would be even harder. Learning in your first language helps.

Bilingual education also helps students to learn how to speak English. Speaking English lets students talk with other people who speak English. This is a very useful skill, because most people in the United States speak English. It is also important that children remember their first language, Spanish, so they can speak with their families and other people in their community.

Teachers know that learning English will help their students get good jobs when they grow up.

PROBLEMS WITH BILINGUAL EDUCATION

Bilingual education helps students in many different ways. It helps teachers give every student an equal chance to learn. However, there are also problems with bilingual education in our schools.

One problem is that students who should be in bilingual classes do not always get into these classes. Sometimes parents do not want their children to go to bilingual classes. Many times, the school does not have money for bilingual programs.

Another problem is that a lot of bilingual programs are only *transitional*. Transitional programs teach children in their first language until the students learn English. After that, the children do not learn in Spanish, only English.

BILINGUALISM IN THE FUTURE

People from many different countries are moving to the United States. The need to speak more than one language is growing. Now telephones and satellites help us talk to people all over the world. These machines make it even more important to know the languages spoken in other countries.

Teachers know that speaking two languages will help their students get good jobs when they become adults. Today students in high school and college often learn a foreign language—sometimes even two. When they are grown-ups, they will be able to do business with people from countries all over the world. They will be able to communicate. Communication helps us stay out of wars. Communication helps us to work together to make the environment better. Communication makes the world a better place to live in—for you and someday for your children, too.

Chapter 5

LEARNING A SECOND LANGUAGE

Bilingual classes use two languages. The *first language* or *primary language* is the language the student knows the best. The first language is sometimes used at home by the parents or grandparents. The *second language* is the language that the student is learning. The second language is the language that the people speak in the new country. For Latino children living in America, Spanish is the first language and English is the second language.

In the classroom, the teacher will use both English and Spanish—but not all bilingual classes are the same. That is, bilingual classes do not always have the same goal. In this chapter, we will learn more about the different goals of bilingual programs. We will also learn a little about what it is like to be a student in a bilingual classroom. Learning another language can be hard, but it can help you speak your first language even better.

TWO KINDS OF BILINGUAL PROGRAMS

There are two kinds of bilingual programs in schools. One kind of program is called *transitional*. The other program is called *maintenance*. In some ways the programs are the same, but in many ways they are different.

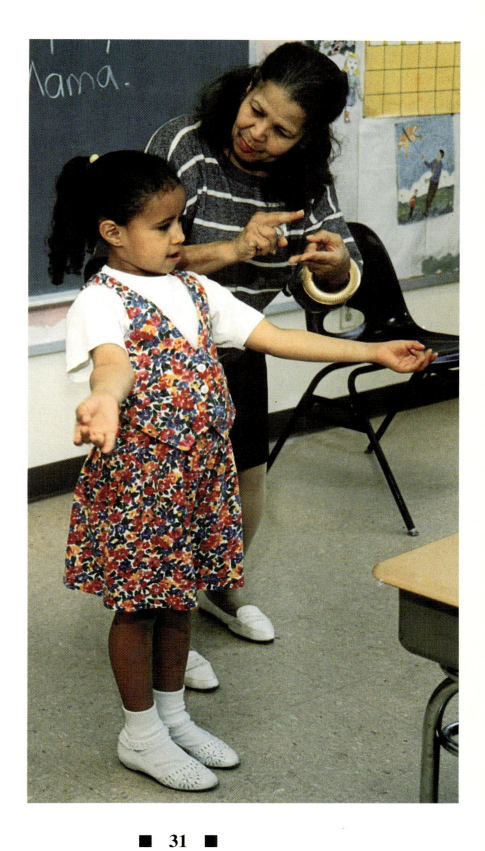

In a bilingual class, students may lead class discussions in English, so the teacher can hear how they are doing.

In a transitional program, children learn their lessons in their first language, like Spanish. Children also learn how to speak English in part of the class. The transitional program teaches students enough English so that they can join an all-English class. The transitional program does not try to teach students better Spanish. The program's goal is to help students get into English-speaking classes.

Maintenance programs teach students to *maintain* both English and Spanish languages. "Maintain" means "keep." Students in maintenance programs keep their Spanish and learn English, too. They learn to speak, read, and write in *both* English and Spanish. Students in bilingual maintenance programs will not move into all-English classes once they learn enough English. They will stay in bilingual classes to maintain their Spanish-speaking abilities.

A BILINGUAL CLASSROOM

Students in both types of programs—transitional and maintenance—learn in English for a part of each school day. They also learn in Spanish. Students in bilingual classes often learn the same thing that students in English-only classes are learning. They study the same subjects. Sometimes they even read the same stories. The main difference is that students in bilingual classes learn mostly in Spanish.

Teachers use different ways of teaching English in bilingual classes. Sometimes they lead class discussions in English. The teachers ask students questions about themselves, and the students answer in English. Sometimes students ask each other questions in English, and they answer in English. These discussions help students practice speaking English with one another. Teachers can hear how the students are doing. If a student is saying something the wrong way, the teacher will hear it and can help the student learn the right way.

Teachers can also help students learn English by letting them work in groups. When students work on a science

Students in bilingual classes may also work in groups, so they can practice together.

project or talk about a story they have read, they practice speaking English. Practicing with each other helps them learn to speak better. It also helps the students understand English when they listen to other people.

Teachers also have students write stories in English, so that they can see English written on paper. Sometimes students learn a list of words. They need to learn how to spell the words and what the words mean. This expands students' vocabulary. A *vocabulary* is all the different words a student knows. A student with a large English vocabulary knows many words in English. A student with a large Spanish vocabulary knows many words in Spanish.

LEARNING ANOTHER LANGUAGE IS HARD WORK

Once a student learns how to speak, read, and write a *primary* (first) language, like Spanish, it seems difficult to learn another one, like English. Learning another language is a lot of work, but it is worth it. Once you learn a second language, you can communicate with many more people. You learn how to say exactly what you want to say. No one will misunderstand you.

Learning a second language also helps you use your first language better. You learn how to say the same thing in many different ways. As you learn more words, you get a bigger vocabulary. Students who speak two languages can use each language better than students who have studied only one language. Many people think that it is good for every student to learn another language.

Chapter 6

IMPORTANT BILINGUAL AMERICANS

Many famous Americans are bilingual in Spanish and English. The bilingual Americans discussed in this chapter have achieved great success. Sometimes the fact that they can speak both English and Spanish is exactly why they have been successful. All of them have helped make America a better place in which to live.

RUDOLFO ANAYA (BORN 1937)

Rudolfo Anaya is one of the most famous Latino authors in the United States. He was born in a little town named Pastura, New Mexico. He studied at the University of New Mexico. His most famous book is *Bless Me, Ultima* (1972). The story takes place in a location much like Anaya's home in New Mexico. In addition to being an award-winning writer, Anaya taught school for several years. Anaya is now the head of the creative writing program at the University of New Mexico. Being able to speak both Spanish and English has made it possible for him to show English-speaking people the world in which he grew up, through writing stories.

Rod Carew (born 1945)

Rod Carew was born in the Panama Canal Zone. He moved to New York when he was seventeen years old. He was offered a professional baseball contract before he graduated from high school. In 1967, he became a member of a major league team, the Minnesota Twins. That year he was named Rookie of the Year. He had a batting average above .300 for fifteen seasons in a row after 1969. He won seven American League batting championships. When he won the Most Valuable Player award, he batted .388. He held the record for most All-Star votes ever received: more than 4 million votes for the 1977 season. He holds 348 career stolen bases, one of the best records in the league.

César Chávez (1927-1993)

César Chávez is the most famous Latino of his generation. He helped thousands of farm workers. He organized unions and worked to get more rights for the workers.

Chávez began his career in 1948. He worked for the Community Service Organization (CSO) in San Jose, California. In ten years, he was director of the CSO for both Arizona and California. In 1962 he left the CSO and headed the United Farm Workers, AFL-CIO. At that time, it was called the United Farmworkers Organizing Committee.

To get people to listen to him, Chávez often used the same ways of protesting that Dr. Martin Luther King, Jr., used for African Americans. Chávez talked on television. He stopped eating until people listened to his message. He organized successful strikes called *huelgas*. A strike, or *huelga*, happens when workers stop working until the bosses listen to them. Chávez led boycotts of crops like grapes. *Boycott* means that people did not buy the grapes. The farm owners could not sell their crops.

These ways of protesting did not hurt people or destroy property. Chávez did these things to make the farm owners listen to him. The workers, he said, should be paid fairly.

Labor leader and Latino rights activist César Chávez used both English and Spanish to communicate with farm workers and farm owners.

They should not have to work longer than anyone else. They should be able to live in clean houses. They should be able to see a doctor when they are sick. Because of César Chávez, many of these things came true. By speaking both Spanish and English, Chávez could learn the farm workers' problems and communicate these problems to people who spoke English. He could organize Latino workers by speaking to them in Spanish.

HENRY G. CISNEROS (BORN 1947)

Henry Cisneros was born in San Antonio, Texas. He studied at Texas A&M University, George Washington University, Harvard University, and the University of Texas. When he grew up, the people voted to make him the mayor of San Antonio. San Antonio is the ninth-largest city in the United States. It also has one of the largest Spanish-speaking populations. Cisneros could help San Antonio's bilingual community because he could speak

Henry Cisneros, former mayor of San Antonio, Texas, and U.S. Secretary of Housing and Urban Development during the Clinton administration.

to people in their own language. When he made decisions on how to run the city, he could understand the needs of *all* the people in the city. Cisneros did such a good job serving his bilingual community that the President of the United States, Bill Clinton, made him Secretary of Housing and Urban Development for the whole country.

JAIME ESCALANTE (BORN 1930)

Jaime Escalante is a teacher of mathematics. He started teaching at Garfield High School in East Los Angeles. He did such a good job that the story of his life was made into a movie, *Stand and Deliver* (1988). Edward James Olmos played the role of Escalante in the film.

Escalante was born and educated in Bolivia, a country in South America. When he moved to the United States, he went to the California State University at Los Angeles. From 1974 to 1990, Escalante worked at Garfield High School. Garfield was a poor high school in the East L.A. *barrio*. Most of the students spoke Spanish as their primary language. The way Escalante taught his classes in both English and Spanish helped students to learn mathematics better than most other students in the United States. Escalante's students learned so well that they often got scholarships to the country's best colleges. Escalante's students loved him very much. If they had not had such a good teacher, they might never have been able to go to college.

Escalante now works in California's capital city, Sacramento. He still teaches mathematics at a high school. He also develops programs to help students learn math. In 1989, the White House gave him the Hispanic Heritage Award. In 1990, the American Institute for Public Service gave him the Jefferson Award.

CAROLINA HERRERA (BORN 1939)

Carolina Herrera is one of the most famous fashion designers in the United States. She became a fashion designer because her friends loved the clothes she made for herself.

Herrera was born in Venezuela. She has designed clothing for such important people as Caroline Kennedy, Jacqueline Kennedy Onassis, and Nancy Reagan. She was elected to the Best-Dressed Hall of Fame, and *Elle* magazine named her one of the Ten Most Elegant Women in the World. In 1987, Herrera received the MODA Award for Top Hispanic Designer. Being able to speak English led to her great success with famous people in America.

ELLEN OCHOA (BORN 1958)

Ellen Ochoa is the first Latina astronaut. She was born in Southern California and received her bachelor's degree in physics from San Diego State University. She earned a master's degree and a Ph.D. in electrical engineering from Stanford University.

Ochoa worked as a research engineer at Sandia National Laboratories and at Ames Research Center, National Aeronautics and Space Administration (NASA). She worked her way up to Information Sciences Division Chief at NASA. She has been awarded the Hispanic Engineer National Achievement Award for the Most Promising Engineer in Government. She also won the Pride Award from the National Hispanic Quincentennial Commission.

PAUL RODRÍGUEZ (BORN 1954?)

Paul Rodríguez is probably the most famous Latino comedian in the United States today. He was born in Mazatlán, Mexico. His parents were immigrant farm workers. He served in the United States Air Force and then entered California State University, Long Beach, in 1977. He was a student of law, but he also took drama classes. His drama teacher recognized his talent and introduced Rodríguez to people who ran a stand-up comedy club. That is how Rodríguez became an actor and comedian.

Ellen Ochoa,
the first Latina
astronaut.

Rodríguez is the host of *El Show de Paul Rodríguez* on the Univisión Spanish-language television network. He has worked in three major television situation comedy series. He has appeared in movies. He heads his own production company. He has produced a comedy album. Even though he is very busy, he still does stand-up comedy in New York City and Atlantic City. Being bilingual means he can be twice as funny—once in Spanish and again in English.

CRISTINA SARALEGUI (BORN 1948)

Cristina Saralegui is the host of the Spanish-language television's most popular daytime show. She came to the United States from Cuba in 1960. Saralegui studied mass communications and creative writing at the University of Miami. She followed in her family's business: magazine and newspaper publishing. She worked for *Vanidades* magazine and later became editor-in-chief of Cosmopolitan-en-Español. Then she left that job to host her own television talk show, called *El Show de Cristina* (the Cristina show).

Cristina's show has been a huge success. Through her radio shows and television programs, she reaches about 6.5 million Spanish speakers in the United States and Latin America every day. Speaking both Spanish and English helps her to do business with people who speak only English in the United States, while entertaining many Spanish speakers throughout the world.

JIMMY SMITS (BORN 1956)

As both a film and television actor, Jimmy Smits has played several very strong Latino roles. He is probably most famous for his part as Victor Sifuentes in the television series *L.A. Law*. In 1989, he starred with Jane Fonda and Gregory Peck in *The Old Gringo*, which was the film version of a novel by world-famous Mexican author Carlos Fuentes. In 1994, he got a starring role in the television series *NYPD Blue*. Jimmy Smits can communicate with both

English and Spanish speakers. This helps him understand the characters that he portrays in movies and on television.

LUIS VALDEZ (BORN 1940)

Luis Valdez is the most important figure in Chicano theater. He founded El Teatro Campesino, a group of Chicano farm workers who put on plays for other farm workers. These plays helped the workers to organize into unions and defend their rights. At one point, Valdez even worked with César Chávez to organize farm workers into a union.

Valdez wrote and directed many famous plays. He is probably most famous for the two films that he wrote and directed: *Zoot Suit* (1982) and *La Bamba* (1987). *Zoot Suit* starred Edward James Olmos as El Pachuco. *La Bamba* starred Lou Diamond Phillips in the role of rock-and-roll singer Ritchie Valens.

Valdez grew up in a family of farm workers. He went to school, but the family had to move all the time. Still, he managed to graduate from high school and studied English and theater at San Jose State College in California. Because he had learned to speak English, he could bring stories from his Spanish-speaking community to life in his plays and in his films.

CARMEN DELGADO VOTAW (BORN 1935)

Carmen Delgado Votaw is the director of the Washington, D.C., office of the Girl Scouts. She helps run this organization, which has helped many girls. In the Girl Scouts, girls learn skills they will need to use when they grow up.

Born in Puerto Rico, Votaw got her bachelor's degree from American University. She held many important positions in women's organizations in the United States and other countries. From 1964 to 1981, Votaw was vice president of the Overseas Education Fund of the League of Women Voters. From 1972 to 1976, she served as the Federal Programs Specialist for the Commonwealth of Puerto Rico in its Washington office. She was also co-chair of the National Advisory Committee on Women, president of the Inter-American Commission of Women of the Organization of American States, and administrative assistant to Congressman Jaime B. Fuster.

Votaw wrote a book called *Puerto Rican Women: Some Biographical Profiles*. She has also written articles for magazines and journals. She has earned many honors and awards, including the Award for Outstanding Achievement from the National Council of Hispanic Women in 1991. Knowing how to speak both Spanish and English has made her a valuable person in the government positions she has held. She can communicate with many different people and understand their concerns and problems.

GLOSSARY

bilingual: Able to speak two languages.

bilingual education: Learning in two languages.

citizen: A person who belongs to a country and has earned the full rights granted by that country.

cognates: Two words in different languages that sound alike.

communicate: Making someone else understand you. You can communicate by talking, listening, smiling, making faces, writing, and reading.

community: People who share a common background or culture.

culture: The parts of a community that make it special and different from other communities.

first language: The language that you know best; the first language you learned.

gender: The state of being either male or female.

immigrant: A person who comes to one country from another country.

Indo-European family of languages: The family of languages that contains English, Spanish, and many other languages spoken in Europe, North America, and South America.

limited-English-speaking: People who may speak some English, but not enough to communicate well in an English-speaking society.

maintenance program: A kind of bilingual program that helps students learn English while they also learn their first language even better.

non-English-speaking: People who speak no English.

patriotism: Pride in your country and where you come from.

primary language: The language that you know best; the first language you learned.

refugee: A person who leaves a country for very serious reasons, like war, poverty, disease, or problems with the government.

second language: The second language that you learned, usually not the language that your parents or grandparents use at home.

Southwest: The part of North America that includes southern California, Arizona, New Mexico, Texas, and northern Mexico.

transitional: Leading from one point to another.

transitional program: A bilingual program that leads from being non-English-speaking (or limited-English-speaking) to being English-speaking.

vocabulary: The words that someone knows and can use in speaking.

MORE ABOUT BEING BILINGUAL

Ada, Alma Flor. *My Name Is María Isabel*. New York: Atheneum, 1993.

Atkin, S. Beth. *Voices from the Fields: Children of Migrant Farmers Tell Their Stories.* Boston: Joy Street Books, 1993.

Augenbraum, Harold, and Ilan Stavans, eds. *Growing Up Latino: Memoirs and Stories.* New York: Houghton Mifflin, 1993.

Brown, Tricia. *Hello, Amigos!* New York: Holt, 1986.

Catalano, Julie. *The Mexican Americans*. New York: Chelsea House, 1988.

Dawson, Mildred Leinweber. *Over Here It's Different: Carolina's Story*. New York: Macmillan, 1993.

De Garza, Patricia. *Chicanos: The Story of Mexican Americans*. New York: J. Messner, 1973.

Dobrin, Arnold. *The New Life— La Vida Nueva: The Mexican Americans Today*. New York: Dodd, Mead, 1971.

Fitch, Robert. *Soy Chicano: I Am Mexican-American*. Mankato, Minn.: Creative Educational Society, 1970.

Galvan, Raúl. *Cuban Americans*. New York: Marshall Cavendish, 1974.

Gernaud, Renée. *The Cuban-Americans*. New York: Chelsea House, 1988.

Grenquist, Barbara. *Cubans*. New York: Franklin Watts, 1991.

Harlan, Judith. *Bilingualism in the United States: Conflict and Controversy*. New York: Franklin Watts, 1991.

Krull, Kathleen. *The Other Side: How Kids in a California Latino Neighborhood Live*. New York: Lodestar Books, 1994.

Kuklin, Susan. *How My Family Lives in America*. New York: Bradbury Press, 1992.

Madison, Winifred. *Maria Luisa*. Philadelphia: J. B. Lippincott, 1971.

Martin, Patricia Miles. *Chicanos: Mexicans in the United States*. New York: Parents' Magazine Press, 1971.

Pinchot, Jane. *The Mexicans in America*. Minneapolis: Lerner Publications, 1989.

Westridge Young Writers Workshop. *Kids Explore America's Hispanic Heritage*. Santa Fe, N.Mex.: J. Muir, 1992.

INDEX

᾿/97